P9-CCP-757

South San Francisco Public Library

3 9048 07641540 9

Countries of the World

United Kingdom

Ro

S.S.F. Public Library
West Orange
840 West Orange Ave.
South San Francisco, CA 94080

DEC   2009

DEMCO

Contents

4 Foreword

7 GEOGRAPHY
Many Nations in One

8 At a Glance
> What's the Weather Like?
> Average Temperature & Rainfall
> Fast Facts
> Physical Map

10 Special Feature: A Fairy-Tale Landscape

11 Special Feature: Rocks in the Sea

13 Special Feature: Pictures in the Chalk

17 NATURE
Wild at Heart

18 At a Glance
> Feathered and Furry Friends
> Species at Risk
> Vegetation & Ecosystems Map

21 Special Feature: The Mighty Oak

23 Special Feature: Cunning Foxes

25 HISTORY
Invaders and Empires

26 At a Glance
> Roman Britain
> Time line
> Historical Map

28 Special Feature: Stonehenge

29 Special Feature: Life on Hadrian's Wall

33 Special Feature: Six Wives for One King

35	Special Feature: The Lady with the Lamp
37	Special Feature Map: War in the South Atlantic

39   PEOPLE & CULTURE
Festivals and Formality

40	At a Glance
	> Living in a City
	> Common Welsh Phrases
	> Population Map
43	Special Feature: Leather on Willow
44	Special Feature: Eisteddfods
46	Special Feature: Public Holidays
47	Special Feature: The Great Bard

49   GOVERNMENT & ECONOMY
Pomp and Ceremony

50	At a Glance
	> Party Politics
	> Trading Partners
	> Political Map
52	Special Feature: How the Government Works
54	Special Feature Map: Industry Map
55	Special Feature: The City Within a City
57	Special Feature: The Eye in the Sky

58	*Add a Little Extra to Your Country Report!*
60	*Glossary*
61	*Bibliography*
	Further Information
62	*Index*
64	*Credits*

Foreword

The United Kingdom is an important global actor that plays a major role in three spheres of influence. Since 1973 it has been a member of the European Union. It heads a Commonwealth of 53 countries, almost all of which were parts of the earlier British Empire. And its governments enjoy a special relationship with the United States, one of Britain's closest allies.

These roles are rooted in Britain's development. In the 1500s and 1600s the nation took a leading part in trade across the Atlantic. In the late 1700s the rise of modern industries made the United Kingdom the world's leading industrial power until the end of the 1900s. And the British built an empire that, at its peak, covered one-third of the world.

However, in the 19th century agriculture began to decline. This was followed by a decline in industry in the 20th century. Today, the economy is dominated by services and the modern United Kingdom remains a leading economic power. The welfare state still provides universal free health care, education, and social security, but there is an unequal distribution of wealth—far more than in the past.

As this book shows, the United Kingdom is a unique country. Politically it is a union of four nations: England, Wales, Scotland, and Northern Ireland. The regions have secured more self-government with the establishment of the Scottish Parliament and Welsh and Northern Irish assemblies. In England regional assemblies have also been set up, although only in Greater London is the assembly elected.

Geographically, Britain's complex geology gives rise to a wide variety of landscapes and a range of habitats for its animal and plant life. These wet and windy islands have also seen 10,000 years of continuous human

settlement that has shaped modern landscapes: forests were cleared, marshes drained, fens reclaimed, fields and roads created, villages established and lost, and cities and suburbs developed.

The British are themselves the creation of waves of invaders and migrants. Early settlers included the Celts, Romans, Anglo-Saxons, Vikings, and Normans. In the Industrial Revolution came the Irish. In the 1950s and 1960s recruits from former colonies in the Caribbean, Africa, and Asia met labor shortages. The more recent arrival of refugees and asylum seekers and of people from other European countries has made the United Kingdom a diverse multicultural society.

▲ **At Oxford University, an ancient heritage is combined with cutting-edge research.**

M. Dunford

Michael Dunford
University of Sussex

Many Nations in One

A TRIP ON THE THAMES River is a trip through British history. In London, the capital city, the river flows beneath Tower Bridge. The bridge carries traffic in and out of the City, London's financial district and a center of the global economy. Five centuries ago, the river looked very different. The heart of the British economy lay 100 miles (160 km) upriver, where the Thames rises in the Cotswold Hills. The area was a leading center of wool production, which helped make Britain a wealthy world power for the first time. London became the busiest port in the world. By the 18th century the city's docks received goods from an empire that stretched around the globe. Today those docks are used for pleasure boats, and the warehouses are apartment buildings.

◀ Tower Bridge rises against the evening sky. It was completed in 1894 with a roadway that opens to allow tall ships to pass through.

WHAT'S THE WEATHER LIKE?

The British are famous for talking about the weather. It is very changeable there. A sunny day can become cold and wet within minutes—and then change back. In general, the climate is mild and wet. It is wettest in the mountains of Scotland and Wales and warmest on England's southern coast. The map opposite shows the physical features of the United Kingdom. Labels on this map and on similar maps throughout the book identify most of the places pictured in each chapter.

Average Temperature & Rainfall

Average High/Low Temperatures; Yearly Rainfall

LONDON (England)
59° F (15° C)/45° F (7° C); 23 in (58 cm)
CAMBRIDGE (England)
57° F (14° C)/42° F (6° C); 22 in (55 cm)
CARDIFF (Wales)
58° F (14° C)/44° F (7° C); 44 in (111 cm)
EDINBURGH (Scotland)
54° F (12° C)/41° F (5° C); 27 in (68 cm)
BELFAST (Northern Ireland)
54° F (12° C)/42° F (6° C); 34 in (86 cm)
STORNOWAY (Scotland, Outer Hebrides)
52° F (11° C)/42° F (6° C); 48 in (123 cm)

Fast Facts

OFFICIAL NAME: United Kingdom of Great Britain and Northern Ireland
FORM OF GOVERNMENT: Constitutional monarchy with parliamentary government
CAPITAL: London
POPULATION: 60,020,000
OFFICIAL LANGUAGES: English; English and Welsh in Wales
MONETARY UNIT: Pound sterling
AREA: 93,635 square miles (242,514 square kilometers)
HIGHEST POINT: Ben Nevis, Scotland, 4,406 feet (1,343 meters)
LOWEST POINT: The Fens, 15 feet (4 meters) below sea level
MAJOR RIVERS: Thames, Severn, Humber, Mersey, Tyne (England); Bann (Northern Ireland); Clyde, Tay, Forth (Scotland); Dee (Wales)
MAJOR LAKES: Windemere, Derwent Water, Ullswater (England); Lough Neagh (Northern Ireland); Loch Lomond, Loch Ness (Scotland)

Orkney
Islands

SHEEP ON BOAT,
page 11

Dunnet Head

Duncansby Head
(John o'Groats)

SHETLAND
ISLANDS

Isle of
Lewis

St. Kilda

Harris

HIGHLANDS

Mainland

Scale same
as main map

Isle of
Skye

Loch
Ness

Cairngorm
Mountains

Dee

UK

Europe

Asia

Ben Nevis
(Highest point in UK)
4,406 ft
1,343 m

SCOTLAND

Tay

Atlantic
Ocean

Africa

Atlantic
Ocean

Loch
Lomond

Firth of Forth

Bass Rock

Glasgow

Edinburgh

Holy Island
(Lindisfarne)

Clyde

GIANT'S CAUSEWAY,
page 10

Southern Uplands

Tweed

North
Channel

Cheviots
Hills

North
Sea

NORTHERN
IRELAND

Lough
Neagh

Belfast

Bann

U N I T E D

Tyne

Newcastle-upon-Tyne

**SHEPHERD
AND SHEEP,**
page 1

Lake
District

Tees

GREAT

North
York Moors

Mourne
Mts.

Isle of
Man

IRELAND

Irish
Sea

BRITAIN

Leeds

Ouse

Humber

MAP KEY

⭐ National capital

● Selected city

+ Elevation

⌇⌇⌇ Canal

Liverpool

Mersey

Manchester

Trent

E N G L A N D

Anglesey

**VIEW ACROSS
VALLEY,**
page 12

Snowdonia

Dee

K I N G D O M

The Fens
(Lowest point in UK)
+ -15 ft
-4 m

The
Broads

miles

100

km

100

Cardigan
Bay

Cambrian Mountains

WALES

Birmingham

WINDMILL,
page 14

East Anglia

TOWER BRIDGE,
pages 2, 6-7

St. George's
Channel

Brecon
Beacons

Severn

**CANAL AND
APARTMENT
BUILDINGS,**
page 15

Oxford

London

**THAMES
BARRIER,**
page 15

Cardiff

Bristol

**OXFORD
UNIVERSITY,**
page 5

Thames

CHANNEL ISLANDS

Alderney

Guernsey

Jersey

Scale same
as main map

FRANCE

Bristol Channel

Exe

Dorset

Southampton

Dover

Isle of
Wight

FRANCE

**WALLED
FIELDS,**
page 12

Cornwall

Dartmoor

Plymouth

Isles of
Scilly

Land's
End

**ST. MICHAEL'S
MOUNT,**
page 10

CHALK HORSE,
page 13

English Channel

Physical Map

How Many Nations?

Many people get confused about the United Kingdom—even those who live there. The nation has four regions: England, Scotland, Wales, and Northern Ireland. England and Scotland are kingdoms; Wales is a principality (a region ruled by a prince), and Northern Ireland is classed as a province. Anyone from the United Kingdom can describe themselves as British, but they may prefer to say that they are English, Scottish, Welsh, or Irish, depending on where they live or where their family comes from.

▲ The islands surrounding Britain include tiny St. Michael's Mount in Cornwall. A pathway joins the island to the shore—but the pathway is flooded every high tide.

An Island Nation

The United Kingdom, or UK, is a group of islands off the northwestern coast of mainland Europe. At its

A FAIRY-TALE LANDSCAPE

The Giant's Causeway is a spectacular rock formation on the coast of Antrim in Northern Ireland. It consists of a mass of six-sided columns of rock. Legend has it that the Irish giant Finn MacCumhaill built the causeway across the sea to attack a Scottish giant named Benandonner. A similar rock formation rises out of the sea on the tiny island of Staffa, where Benandonner lived. In fact, the causeway was formed 60 million years ago when melted rock from deep within the Earth escaped through cracks and cooled into the unique columns.

▲ A third of a million people visit the Giant's Causeway every year.

ROCKS IN THE SEA

The Outer Hebrides are a chain of 120 islands off the northwestern coast of Scotland. They include Lewis and Harris, as well as St. Kilda, some 40 miles (64 km) to the west. After St. Kilda, the next land is Newfoundland, Canada, nearly 2,000 miles (3,200 km) across the Atlantic.

The islands have harsh weather and poor soil, but people have lived there for at least 5,000 years. Ancient islanders built the mysterious standing stones of Callanish on Lewis. Today's islanders are mainly farmers and fishers. They are among the few people who still speak Gaelic, an old Scottish language.

▲ Sheep are loaded onto a boat in Lewis. Their wool is made into a thick cloth called tweed. The dye on their backs shows if they have mated.

closest point, it is just 18 miles (30 km) away from France. Many people think that Great Britain is a country, but in fact it is the largest island of the United Kingdom; it is about the same size as the state of Oregon. Great Britain contains England, Wales, and Scotland. Northern Ireland is the northeastern part of Ireland, a large island to the west. The rest of Ireland makes up the Republic of Ireland, a separate nation.

Together, Great Britain and Ireland make up the British Isles, which also include hundreds of smaller islands around the coasts. Many of these islands, such as the Isle of Wight, Lundy, and Anglesey, are part of the United Kingdom. Scotland has more islands than any other part of the country. They include the Hebrides, Orkneys, and Shetland Isles. The Shetlands are the northernmost part of Britain; they are closer to Norway than they are to England.

In the Hills

Much of the north and west of the United Kingdom is covered in high ground. The most dramatic mountains are in the Scottish Highlands, the English Lake District, Snowdonia in Wales, and Mourne in Northern Ireland. These uplands were shaped in the last Ice Age, when glaciers a mile thick covered the land. The ice slowly gouged out the landscape, creating knife-edge mountain ridges separated by deep valleys.

▲ A sheep farmer looks across a wide valley carved by a glacier in Snowdonia, a mountain range in Wales.

▼ Many of the stone walls dividing Cornwall into small fields for livestock are centuries old.

Britain's mountains are cold and wet, and their thin soil is not good for growing crops. The few small farms that cling to the lower slopes can only raise tough breeds of sheep and cattle. England has fewer high mountains than either Scotland or Wales.

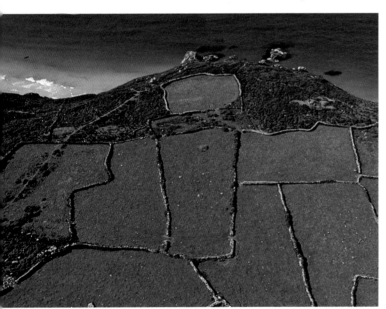

Lake Lands

After the glaciers of the Ice Age melted, many valleys flooded, creating lakes. They created dramatic scenery in the Lake District in northwest

England and in the Scottish Highlands, where the lakes are called lochs.

Some lochs are connected to the sea and have a mixture of fresh and salt water. Lochs tend to be long and narrow, and some are very deep. For example, Loch Ness is 788 feet (240 m) deep—deeper than much of the sea that surrounds Scotland. Loch Ness's great depth has led to a world-famous myth. Some people believe that a giant monster lives in the depths. There have been several sightings of "Nessie," as the Loch Ness monster is nicknamed. But biologists do not think it would be possible for any large animals to find enough food in the loch's waters to survive.

Green and Pleasant

England is the largest country in the United Kingdom, and the most crowded and wealthy. Nine out of ten British people live in England. Much of the English countryside is gently rolling hills made of chalk or limestone (stone made from the remains of tiny seashells).

PICTURES IN THE CHALK

Much of southern and eastern England lies above chalk. For thousands of years people have cleared away layers of soil to make giant chalk pictures, usually of horses and men.

The oldest surviving chalk figure is the 374-foot-long (114-m) Uffington White Horse in Oxfordshire. It was made 3,000 years ago but no one knows why. Perhaps it was an offering to the ancient gods or showed a tribal boundary. Most chalk horses are only a couple of hundred years old. The most recent one was made in Folkestone, Kent, to celebrate the New Year in 2000.

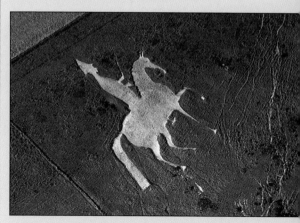

▲ The Osmington White Horse in Dorset and other chalk figures were covered during World War II, so that German pilots could not use their white glow to navigate.

▼ A windmill stands beside a waterway in the Norfolk marshes. Norfolk, Suffolk, and Cambridgeshire—a region known as East Anglia—are mostly flat, so strong winds blow over them from the North Sea.

An Artificial Landscape

The flatlands of eastern England have landscapes that have been shaped by people. The shallow pools and waterways of the Broads in Norfolk and Suffolk, for example, were created several hundred years ago. Rivers and the sea flooded pits and ditches left by people digging peat. Peat is a soft form of coal that was burned widely as a fuel.

The Fens in Cambridgeshire are farmlands made from drained marshes. The area is below sea level, and water slowly leaks back onto the land. In the 1700s, windmills pumped out the water to drain the marshes. Today, electric pumps keep the Fens dry.

Landscape under Threat

The long coastlines of the United Kingdom are under constant threat of flooding and erosion (being washed away). In low-lying areas, the sea has already taken over land that used to be dry. The town of Dunwich, which was a flourishing port on the Suffolk coast in the

1200s, has been almost completely washed away. The sea eats away the east coast at a rate of one yard (90 cm) a year in some places. Homeowners watch over the years as their yards fall into the sea—and then move before their houses follow.

High tides often surge up the mouths of large rivers, such as the Severn. The water flows over the banks and causes floods. In 1984, the world's largest moveable flood barrier was built across the Thames River to protect London from a large tidal surge.

City Living

Almost ninety percent of the British live in towns and cities. Many of the modern cities formed because of what lay beneath them. Birmingham, Newcastle-upon-Tyne, and Swansea, for example, became industrial centers because of nearby coalfields and iron-ore mines. The cities are connected by a network of canals.

▲ Birmingham is the hub of the canal network. The city has more canals than Venice, Italy.

▼ The gates of the Thames Barrier are raised to protect the city from storm surges.

Wild
at
Heart

I N THE SCOTTISH HIGHLANDS, the red deer stag is known as the "Monarch of the Glen." *Glen* is the Scottish word for "valley." The stag gets its name from its crown of antlers, worthy of a monarch, or king. Red deer are Britain's largest wild animals, yet the moorlands (high treeless areas) where they live are not quite as wild as they seem. Like most British landscapes, they have been changed by people. The moors were once covered in forest, the deer's natural habitat. They were cleared thousands of years ago by ancient farmers. The red deer, like many other species, has adapted to this new environment. The United Kingdom is very crowded, and there are few truly wild places left. The most successful wildlife species are those that can live alongside people.

◀ A young red deer stag stands majestically among the heather of a Scottish moor. In North America, red deer are known as elk or wapiti.

FEATHERED AND FURRY FRIENDS

The British are great animal lovers. Many of them keep pets, and their country is home to 14 million cats and dogs—one for every four humans. Many British people live in towns, so they encourage wildlife to visit their yards by putting out food and providing birdhouses.

British people often join conservation organizations, such as the Royal Society for the Protection of Birds (RSPB), which was founded in 1889 and is now one of the largest organizations of its kind in the world.

The map opposite shows vegetation zones—or what grows where—in the United Kingdom. They range from coastal mud flats and sand banks, through marshes, woodland, and meadows, to bare moors. Since the 1950s, many of these habitats have been protected as National Parks.

▶ **The Farne Islands, in the northeast of England, are a great place to see puffins.**

Species at Risk

About four-fifths of the United Kingdom is countryside, ranging from farmland to wild mountains and moors. However, British wildlife has long been under threat from human activities. In the 19th century, pollution became a major problem, caused both by using chemicals in farming and by industrial waste. The Wildlife and Countryside Act was passed in 1981 to protect wildlife. As well as government agencies, a number of conservation organizations such as the National Trust and the RSPB also work to protect the environment.

Species at risk include:
> Bittern (bird)
> Common otter
> Corncrake (bird)
> Fen raft spider
> Great crested newt
> Grey partridge
> House sparrow
> Lady's slipper orchid
> Marsh harrier (bird)
> Natterjack toad
> Northern right whale
> Nightjar (bird)
> Pearl mussel
> Pink sea fan (coral)
> Porbeagle (shark)
> Red kite (bird)
> Red squirrel
> Stone curlew (bird)
> Wood lark

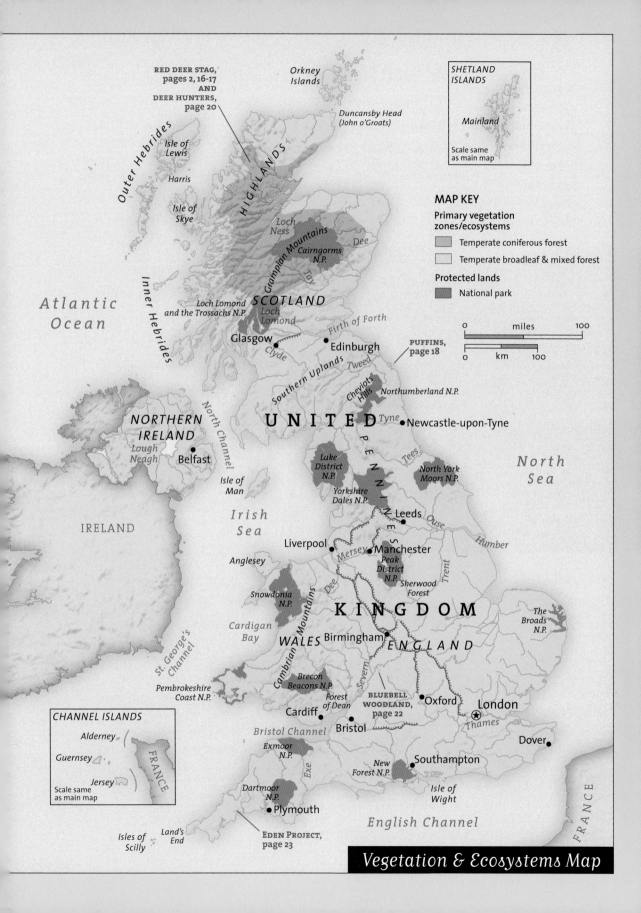

RED DEER STAG,
pages 2, 16–17
AND
DEER HUNTERS,
page 20

Orkney
Islands

Duncansby Head
(John o'Groats)

SHETLAND
ISLANDS

Mainland

Scale same
as main map

Outer Hebrides

Isle of
Lewis

Harris

Isle of
Skye

HIGHLANDS

Loch
Ness

Grampian Mountains

Cairngorms
N.P.

Dee

MAP KEY

**Primary vegetation
zones/ecosystems**

Temperate coniferous forest

Temperate broadleaf & mixed forest

Protected lands

National park

Inner Hebrides

Atlantic
Ocean

Loch Lomond
and the Trossachs N.P.

Tay

SCOTLAND

Loch
Lomond

Glasgow

Clyde

Edinburgh

Firth of Forth

PUFFINS,
page 18

miles

0   100

0   km   100

Southern Uplands

Tweed

Cheviots
Hills

Northumberland N.P.

NORTHERN
IRELAND

North Channel

U N I T E D

Tyne

Newcastle-upon-Tyne

Lough
Neagh

Belfast

Isle of
Man

Lake
District
N.P.

Tees

North
Sea

IRELAND

Irish
Sea

Yorkshire
Dales N.P.

North York
Moors N.P.

P
E
N
N
I
N
E
S

Leeds

Ouse

Humber

Anglesey

Liverpool

Mersey

Manchester

Peak
District
N.P.

Sherwood
Forest

Trent

St. George's Channel

Snowdonia
N.P.

Cambrian Mountains

Dee

K I N G D O M

The
Broads
N.P.

Cardigan
Bay

WALES

Birmingham

E N G L A N D

Pembrokeshire
Coast N.P.

Brecon
Beacons N.P.

Forest
of Dean

Severn

BLUEBELL
WOODLAND,
page 22

Oxford

London

CHANNEL ISLANDS

Cardiff

Bristol

Thames

Dover

Alderney

Guernsey

FRANCE

Jersey

Bristol Channel

Exmoor
N.P.

Exe

New
Forest N.P.

Southampton

Scale same
as main map

Dartmoor
N.P.

Isle of
Wight

Isles of
Scilly

Land's
End

Plymouth

EDEN PROJECT,
page 23

English Channel

FRANCE

Vegetation & Ecosystems Map

Mountains and Moorlands

Rugged mountains are some of the few British habitats to remain untouched by humans. The peaks of the remote Scottish Highlands are home to the golden eagle, the largest bird in Britain. The bird's wing span of around 7 feet (2 m) enables it to remain in the sky for hours and to drop on its prey at speeds of up to 80 miles (128 km) an hour.

▼ Scottish deer hunters stalk a stag across a glen. They are dressed in traditional tweed clothes, which makes them camouflaged—allowing them to blend in with their background.

The eagle's prey includes rabbits, hares, and even baby deer. The fawns take cover from attack by hiding under their mothers. The eagle also attacks other birds—particularly the red grouse. The grouse lives on moors and feeds on heather, one of the few plants to flourish in the poor soil. Grouse are hunted by humans, too. Since the 1800s, Scots have organized shooting parties on the moors. The grouse season starts every August 12, which hunters call the Glorious Twelfth.

Coasts and Cliffs

With 7,700 miles (12,429 km) of shoreline, coastal habitats are a major part of Britain's environment. They range from tall cliffs to pebble beaches and muddy marshes, and are home to a variety of wildlife.

THE MIGHTY OAK

The oak has played an important part in Britain's history. The trees produce very strong timber, which was used in many of the United Kingdom's historic buildings. Oak was also used to make the great sailing ships that established the country as a mighty sea power in the 1600s.

Many oak forests were planted at that time to provide timber for the growing Royal Navy. The remains of these forests are still dotted around the country. One of the largest remnants is the remote Forest of Dean in Gloucestershire.

The oak was sacred to the Druids, ancient British religious leaders. The tree has also become a symbol of strength and longevity. It often grows to a great age: one of the oldest trees in Britain is the Major

▲ Although the oak grows in many countries, the English regard it as their national tree.

Oak, which is around 800 years old. This huge tree is in Sherwood Forest near Nottingham, which is also famous as the home of the legendary outlaw Robin Hood.

More than half of all Europe's gray seals live on rocky shores and islands off the Scottish and Welsh coasts. The seaside's most common residents are herring gulls—known locally just as seagulls. These birds scavenge for scraps thrown from ships or among trash in coastal towns. Nowhere is far from the coast, and seagulls often fly inland. They are an increasing pest in some cities, where they are jokingly nicknamed "land gulls."

Seabirds roost in large groups called colonies. They are often sited on steep cliffs, out of reach of predators. A famous colony on Bass Rock, off the southeast coast of Scotland, is home to 100,000 birds.

Forests and Woodland

About 5,000 years ago, the center of the United Kingdom was covered with thick forests; today, woodland covers only about 10 percent of the land. It ranges from pine forests in Scotland to broad-leaf forests of trees such as oak, beech, birch, ash, sycamore, hazel, and sweet chestnut.

The woodlands are home to animal species such as deer, badgers, and foxes. Squirrels are also common. Gray squirrels were brought to the UK from North America in 1876. Since then the larger grays have almost driven the native red squirrel out of England and Wales. It survives mainly in the Scottish pine forests.

▲ An injured badger recovers at a special clinic for wild animals. Such clinics are quite common in the UK.

▼ The woods of Britain are home to half of all the world's bluebells.

Adapting to Changes

Over centuries, Britain's wildlife has adapted to new habitats. The woodlands and marshes have given way to fields, hedges, and gardens. Moles, mice, and voles live in farmland, where they attract predators such as foxes. Robins, blackbirds, tits, and many other birds have settled in gardens.

One favorite British species is actually a foreign invader. There

were no rabbits in Britain until the Romans brought them from Europe in A.D. 43. The Romans bred rabbits for food, but the animals soon escaped. Now rabbits are among the country's most commonly seen wild animals.

Concrete Jungles

Britain's cities are also home to wildlife. Pigeons were once bred for food, but they now live wild. They have been a common sight in London's streets for at least 600 years. Tourists once enjoyed feeding the pigeons in places like Trafalgar Square. That has now been banned to try to drive away the pesky birds. Pigeon-hunting peregrine falcons are now a common sight in London, too. They do not nest on cliffs, but on the ledges of high-rise buildings. The falcons are just the latest of British species to adapt to the changing landscape around them.

CUNNING FOXES

Foxes are some of the most adaptable wild animals in Britain. Originally at home in fields and remote woods, they now live much closer to people. But the relationship is often uneasy.

Foxes are hunters and scavengers. For centuries they have helped themselves to chickens and ducks from poultry farms. For this reason, they have been regarded as pests by Britain's farmers, who, until recently, hunted and trapped them.

The number of foxes has remained high, however, because the animals have moved into towns and city suburbs. They scavenge food from garbage cans. It is now common to meet a fox while walking along Britain's city streets at night. City foxes are not tame, but they have grown used to their human neighbors.

▼ The plastic domes of the Eden Project in Cornwall house plants from tropical jungles and other warm parts of the world.

Invaders
and
Empires

T HE UP HELLY-AA, OR FIRE FESTIVAL, is one of the most dramatic reminders of the United Kingdom's varied past. It is held every January in Lerwick, on the Shetland Islands. The festival ends with a full-size Viking longship being set ablaze. The Vikings were seafaring warriors from Scandinavia—160 miles (250 km) east of Shetland. Beginning in the eighth century, Vikings raided Britain's coasts and islands, and many stayed behind.

The Vikings were just one wave of invaders who shaped early Britain. Later, the rulers of England brought Wales, Scotland, and Ireland together to create the United Kingdom, a single powerful nation. Its influence is reflected by the fact that English is the most widespread language in the world today.

◀ **A torchlit procession arrives at a longship before it is set alight at the Up Helly-Aa in Lerwick. The procession is made up of exactly 902 men, many in Viking costumes.**

ROMAN BRITAIN

The first Britons were the Picts, who arrived in Britain about ten thousands years ago. In the 8th century B.C. the Celts arrived from Europe and pushed the Picts north into Scotland.

In A.D. 43, the Romans invaded the island. Within four years England was in Roman hands and by A.D. 78 so, too, was Wales. Only the Picts in Scotland were undefeated.

The Romans ruled over the many British tribes. They built cities, forts, and a network of roads—some of which are still part of the country's road system. The British grew wealthy under Roman rule and began to enjoy their rulers' advanced way of life. Towns had bathhouses and sewers, and large villas were built in the countryside.

By the 400s the Roman Empire was weakening. The Romans pulled out of Britain—but their influence remained.

▼ Carvings of three Roman gods from a fort in northeast England. The sculptor has given the figures warm coats to keep out the cold northern weather.

Time line

This chart shows the approximate dates for some of the major periods and ruling families in the history of the United Kingdom from the arrival of the Romans in the first century B.C. to the present day.

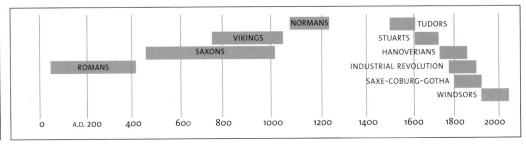

NORMANS
VIKINGS
SAXONS
ROMANS
TUDORS
STUARTS
HANOVERIANS
INDUSTRIAL REVOLUTION
SAXE-COBURG-GOTHA
WINDSORS

0   A.D. 200   400   600   800   1000   1200   1400   1600   1800   2000

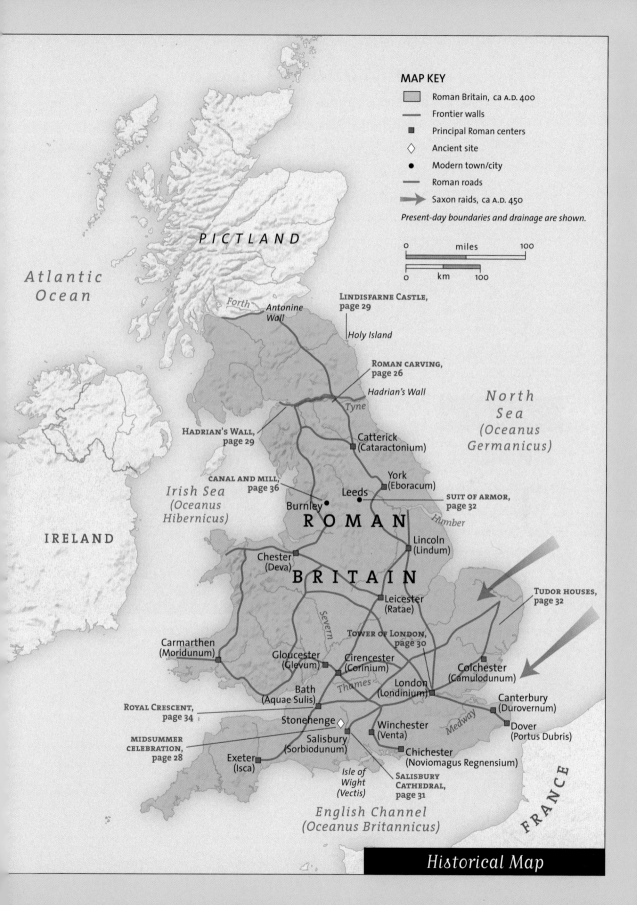

MAP KEY

Roman Britain, ca A.D. 400

Frontier walls

Principal Roman centers

Ancient site

Modern town/city

Roman roads

Saxon raids, ca A.D. 450

Present-day boundaries and drainage are shown.

miles
0   100

km
0   100

Atlantic
Ocean

PICTLAND

Forth

Antonine
Wall

LINDISFARNE CASTLE,
page 29

Holy Island

ROMAN CARVING,
page 26

Hadrian's Wall

Tyne

HADRIAN'S WALL,
page 29

Catterick
(Cataractonium)

North
Sea
(*Oceanus
Germanicus*)

CANAL AND MILL,
page 36

York
(Eboracum)

SUIT OF ARMOR,
page 32

*Irish Sea
(Oceanus
Hibernicus)*

Burnley

Leeds

Humber

R O M A N

IRELAND

Lincoln
(Lindum)

Chester
(Deva)

B R I T A I N

Severn

Leicester
(Ratae)

TUDOR HOUSES,
page 32

Carmarthen
(Moridunum)

Gloucester
(Glevum)

TOWER OF LONDON,
page 30

Cirencester
(Corinium)

Colchester
(Camulodunum)

Bath
(Aquae Sulis)

Thames

London
(Londinium)

Canterbury
(Durovernum)

ROYAL CRESCENT,
page 34

Stonehenge

Winchester
(Venta)

Medway

Dover
(Portus Dubris)

**MIDSUMMER
CELEBRATION,**
page 28

Salisbury
(Sorbiodunum)

Exeter
(Isca)

Chichester
(Noviomagus Regnensium)

*Isle of
Wight
(Vectis)*

**SALISBURY
CATHEDRAL,**
page 31

*English Channel
(Oceanus Britannicus)*

FRANCE

Historical Map

Angles and Saxons

After the Romans withdrew from Britain in 410, England and Wales broke up into small kingdoms organized around local rulers. Scotland and Ireland had never been conquered by the Romans. Celtic peoples known as the Picts lived in Scotland, and the Scoti lived in Ireland. When the Scoti invaded Scotland, they gave their name to that country.

By the 6th century, German peoples known as Angles, Jutes, and Saxons were moving to Britain in large numbers from northern Europe. Over the following century, they settled most of England and parts of lowland Scotland. The Angles gave their name

STONEHENGE

Stonehenge in Wiltshire, England, is one of the world's most famous ancient monuments. The stone circle was built in stages between about 3,000 and 1,100 B.C. But no one knows exactly what the monument was for. Parts of it line up with sunrise at the Summer Solstice, the longest day of the year. Perhaps it was an observatory to check the timing of religious ceremonies.

Whatever it was, Stonehenge was clearly important to its builders. It would have taken hundreds of workers to transport and raise the huge stones. The largest weigh 50 tons (43,550 kg)—more than three school buses—

▲ Every year a party is held inside Stonehenge as revelers wait for the midsummer sunrise.

and come from 20 miles (30 km) away. The smaller stones weigh 4 tons each. They had to be brought by river and overland 240 miles (385 km) from southwest Wales.

LIFE ON HADRIAN'S WALL

When the Romans were unable to subdue the tribes of Scotland, they built a barrier to keep them out of the empire. The 73-mile (118-km) wall was completed in A.D. 126. It is now named for Hadrian, the emperor at the time.

The 16 forts along Hadrian's Wall were defended by soldiers who patrolled the wall and guarded the crossing points—merchants often passed through. The soldiers came from as far away as what are now Romania and Greece. They were unused to the cold, wet weather on the wall. But the soldiers were well cared for. They received many supplies, such as olive oil and wine, to remind them of home.

▲ Hadrian's Wall was the most long-lasting frontier of Roman Britain. Another wall was built farther north, but it was only occupied briefly.

to England, and English people from this time (as well as the German dialect they spoke) are known as Anglo-Saxon. The original Celtic inhabitants of England were driven west into Cornwall and Wales.

In the 6th and 7th centuries, missionaries from Europe converted the Anglo-Saxons to Christianity. Saint Patrick had already brought the religion to Ireland in A.D. 432. Saint Columba then spread the faith to Scotland and northern England in the 500s. Meanwhile, Saint Augustine was sent from Rome, the center of the Catholic Church, to convert the people of southern England.

▼ Lindisfarne Castle rises above Holy Island in northeast England. The island was home to a monastery founded by followers of Saint Columba in A.D. 635. The castle was built from the monastery's stones.

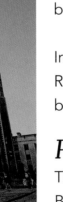

By tradition, if ravens leave the Tower of London, the kingdom will fall. To make sure they stay, the birds' wings are painlessly clipped.

▼ The Tower of London was one of dozens of strong stone castles built by the Normans.

A Series of Conquerors

Vikings raided Britain's coasts through the 900s, and after 1016 England was ruled by a Danish Viking named Canute. According to legend, Canute's followers believed that the king had magical godlike powers. To show that he did not, Canute commanded the tide not to come in—obviously the water kept on rising. Soon after Danish rule ended, England was conquered by another group of Vikings, this time Normans from northern France. They invaded in 1066.

The Norman kings made sure that they held on to power by building castles throughout the country. The Norman rulers spoke French, which became mixed with Anglo-Saxon. That mix formed the beginnings of the modern English language.

England's Norman kings conquered Ireland (1171) and Wales (1289). Like the Romans before them, however, they were beaten back by the Scots.

Plague and War

The 1300s were a disastrous century. The Black Death, a plague spread by rats, struck

England in 1348. It killed a third of the population. As the country began to recover in the early 1400s, England's nobles began to fight among themselves. Two powerful families battled over who should be the next king. The Lancasters had a red rose as their family symbol, while their rivals, the Yorks, had a white rose. Their 30-year conflict is known as the Wars of the Roses.

Tudor Changes

In 1485 the Welsh noble Henry Tudor ended the fighting by claiming the crown for himself. He became Henry VII, the first of five Tudor monarchs. They were some of the most famous in English history, including Henry VIII, Mary I—the first queen of England—and Elizabeth I.

The Tudors chose a family symbol of a red and white rose, as a sign that the warring nobles should come together. During the long peace that followed, England grew into a wealthy and powerful nation.

The Tudors shaped England's future. A key change came when Henry VIII split from the Roman Catholic Church. The king left Roman Catholicism so he could grant himself a divorce and remarry—in the end he got married six times! But Henry also wanted to

▲ The nave—main hall—of Salisbury Cathedral was finished in 1280. The 13th and 14th centuries were a great age of cathedral building in southern Britain.

increase his power and wealth by seizing the property of the Church.

The courts of Henry and his daughter Queen Elizabeth I became centers of fashion, learning, and the arts. Elizabeth also laid the foundations of the British Empire. She expanded the navy and sent explorers to set up trading posts around the world. The country began to challenge the power of other European nations. In 1588 Elizabeth's navy defeated a strong Spanish invasion fleet, known as the Armada.

▲ These timber and plaster houses in Suffolk were built in Tudor times.

▼ Henry VIII's suit of armor from 1520 gets polished. The suit is valued at $40 million.

Two into One

Elizabeth had no children. When she died, the throne passed to her cousin, King James VI of Scotland. He became King James I of England, uniting the two countries for the first time. However, James inherited an unstable kingdom. Henry's split from the Roman Catholic Church had triggered religious trouble. The official church was Protestant, but many people wanted to remain Catholic. Several Protestant groups also disagreed about how to worship.

SIX WIVES FOR ONE KING

King Henry VIII is famous for having six wives—and for executing two of them. Why would he do such a thing? He was obsessed with producing a son and heir.

Henry's first wife, Catherine of Aragon, was older than he. When she had no sons, Henry turned his attentions to Anne Boleyn.

When Anne became pregnant, Henry needed to annul, or cancel, his marriage to Catherine in order to marry Anne. It became clear that the pope would not end the marriage, so Henry set up a new church—the Church of England—which did. He married Anne, but their baby was a girl—the future Elizabeth I. Still without a son, Henry had Anne beheaded. Two weeks later, he married Jane Seymour. She gave birth to the future Edward VI, but she soon died. Henry went on to have three more wives: Anne of Cleves, Catherine Howard—whom the king also had executed—and Catherine Parr.

▲ The letter asking the pope to annul Henry's first marriage carries the wax seals of all 85 English nobles who signed it. The seals showed that the signatures were real.

One powerful group were the Puritans, who wanted to "purify" their religion of all influences other than God Himself. Some Puritans left England so they could practice their religion freely, many settling mostly in the Netherlands and in America. In England, religious differences also caused trouble between the king and Parliament, which made England's laws. A civil war broke out that was won by Parliament. In 1649 King Charles I was beheaded on the orders of Parliament, which now ran the country. It was only in 1660 that the English asked Charles's son, Charles II, to become the next king.

The Rise of Parliament

In 1701 Parliament passed new laws to try to end religious tension in England. They stated that only a Protestant could become king or queen. But in 1714 the English crown passed to a German noble who became George I. The new king could not speak English. There were 41 other people that were closer relatives of the last monarch, but he was the closest Protestant. Since then, all British monarchs have been related to him.

With a foreign king, Parliament began to play a larger role in governing Britain. George appointed a prime minister to govern on his behalf. The first political parties emerged. Only rich landowners could run for Parliament or vote in elections. Most Britons had no say in the running of the country.

▼ The Royal Crescent in the historic town of Bath, is a fine example of the architecture of the Georgian period—the reign of George I to George IV in the 1700s and early 1800s.

THE LADY WITH THE LAMP

The pioneering British nurse Florence Nightingale (1820–1910) became known for her work in the Crimean War fought between Britain and its allies and Russia (1854–56). Reports reached Britain about the conditions in which wounded soldiers were being cared for on the battlefield in Russia. More were dying from disease than from their injuries. Nightingale gathered a group of nurses and set out to work in the hospitals there.

She ensured that the filthy wards were thoroughly cleaned and personally looked after the wounded soldiers. She became known as the Lady with the Lamp *(pictured)* because of her nighttime rounds of the wards. Her changes greatly reduced the number of deaths.

Nightingale returned home as a heroine. She went on to found a school for nurses and to campaign for better health care. This pioneering nurse received many honors and is seen as the founder of modern nursing.

Trade, Industry, and Empire

By the 1800s Britain was one of the most powerful nations in the world. During the reign of Queen Victoria from 1837 to 1901—the longest of any British monarch —trade generated immense wealth. The country built up a huge overseas empire, although it had lost some of its North American colonies in 1783, after the American Revolution. Britain controlled all of Canada and large parts of India, Africa, and the Caribbean, as well as Australia and New Zealand in the Pacific.

The Victorians—the British during Victoria's rule—had the most advanced industry of their time. Technological breakthroughs

▼ A stamp from Trinidad and Tobago, an island nation near Venezuela, carries a picture of Elizabeth II. The country became a British colony in 1899. The queen remained its head of state until 1976.

encouraged industry, and there were ample raw materials and inexpensive labor. As people moved to find work in factories, urban areas grew rapidly. In the 19th century new laws ensured that the new towns and cities were represented in Parliament. By 1885 all working men were given the vote. Women were not able to vote until 1919.

A Troubled Century

The first half of the 20th century was a time of setbacks for Britain. Hundreds of thousands of soldiers were killed in World War I (1914–18) and World War II (1939–45). Many civilians also died when German airplanes bombed Britain's cities during World War II. Britain could no longer afford its overseas empire. Most of its colonies became independent.

▼ **A cotton mill in Burnley, Lancashire, stands unused beside a canal. In the early 1800s Burnley was one of the centers of the Industrial Revolution, like other towns in northwest England. The canal carried cotton to the port of Liverpool for export abroad.**

WAR IN THE SOUTH ATLANTIC

In 1982 British and Argentine troops fought each other in the Falkland Islands War. The windswept Falkland Islands are in the Atlantic Ocean, about 300 miles (480 km) off the coast of Argentina, in South America. Even though the islands are some 8,000 miles (12,874 km) from the United Kingdom, the British made them a British colony in 1833. Today's 2,300 islanders are descendants of British settlers from this time.

The Argentines have always considered that the islands, which they call the Malvinas, belonged to them. On April 2, 1982, the Argentine president General Galtieri ordered an invasion of the Falklands. His government was unpopular, and he hoped that the invasion would gain him support. However, when British troops retook the islands ten weeks later, Galtieri had to resign. The popularity of British prime minister Margaret Thatcher soared, and the islands have remained British ever since. Many people in Britain, however, began to wonder why the country holds on to such remote colonies.

▲ A signpost at Stanley, the capital of the remote Falkland Islands, points to many distant places.

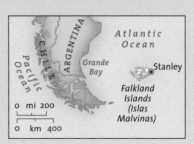

Meanwhile, in Ireland resentment at British rule brought the country close to civil war. In 1920 the country was split in two; the south became independent in 1922. Northern Ireland stayed in the United Kingdom. Beginning in the 1960s, divisions between Northern Ireland's Protestants (who favored union with Britain) and Roman Catholics (who wanted union with Ireland) erupted into terrorism—a period now known as "the Troubles." Peace was not restored until the 1990s.

Festivals
and
Formality

EVERY AUGUST, THE UNITED KINGDOM'S biggest party takes place in west London. The Notting Hill Carnival attracts more than a million people from across the country. Today, Carnival fills 3 miles (5 km) of road, but when it began about 50 years ago, the party fit in a town hall. Carnival is a celebration of the culture of the Caribbean people who came to work in London and other British cities in the 1950s. Many ended up in Notting Hill, then a run-down area. Since then, things have changed. In the 1970s African and Indian people moved in. Their influence can now be seen among the steel-drum bands and the speakers blasting out dance music at Carnival. No matter where you are from, you're invited to Carnival!

◀ There are several parades during the Notting Hill Carnival. Local residents prepare all year so they can make an impact on the big day.

LIVING IN A CITY

Britain is home to 60 million people. Thanks to the Industrial Revolution, it was the first large country to have more people living in cities than in the countryside. Today, 80 percent of Britons live in cities and most of the others live in giant suburbs that sprawl outward from most cities.

The ten main metropolitan areas alone contain 19 million people—and rising. The largest city is London. It is home to 7 million people, who crowd into 610 square miles (1,579 sq. km). This also means that the capital is the most crowded place in the country. There are plans to extend London to the east. By far the largest Scottish city is Glasgow; it is home to one in three Scots.

▶ **Most British cities, such as Liverpool, have busy shopping districts at their centers.**

Common Welsh Phrases

While English is the official language of the United Kingdom, in Wales a fifth of the population also speaks Welsh. All schoolchildren there have to study the language until they are 16. Here are a few words and phrases in Welsh. Give them a try:

Bore da (BORreh da) Good morning
Prynhawn da (pnaown da) Good afternoon
Noswaith dda (NOSSwythe dha) Good evening
Nos da (nos da) Good night
Helo (heLO) Hello
Croeso (CROY-so) Welcome
Hwyl (hooil) Goodbye
Penblwydd hapus (PENblwidh HAPiss) Happy birthday
Pob lwc (pawb look) Good luck

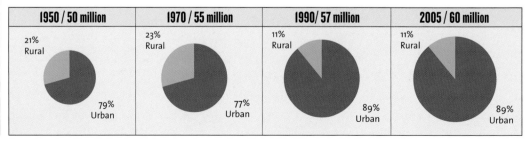

1950 / 50 million	1970 / 55 million	1990 / 57 million	2005 / 60 million
21% Rural · 79% Urban	23% Rural · 77% Urban	11% Rural · 89% Urban	11% Rural · 89% Urban

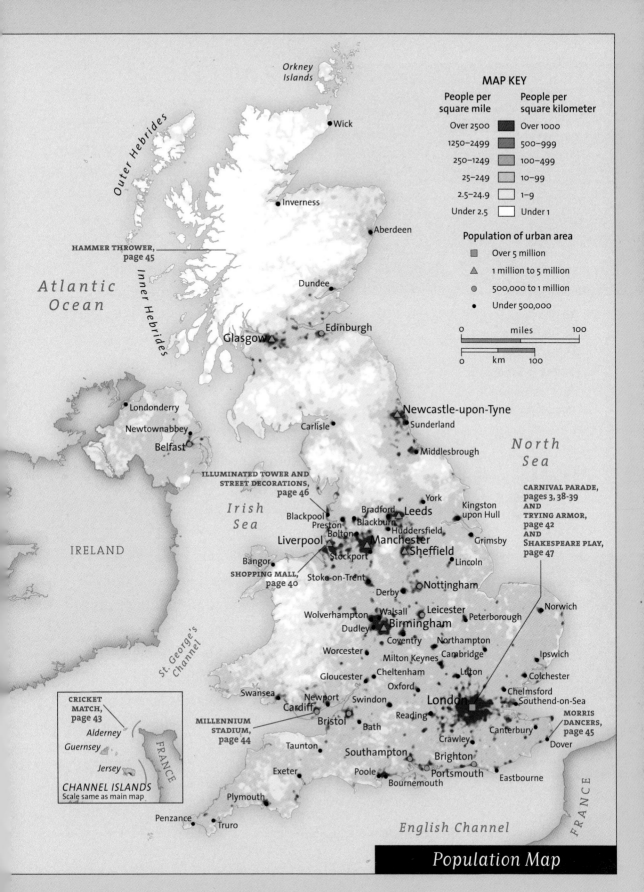

Population Map

MAP KEY

People per square mile	People per square kilometer
Over 2500	Over 1000
1250–2499	500–999
250–1249	100–499
25–249	10–99
2.5–24.9	1–9
Under 2.5	Under 1

Population of urban area

■ Over 5 million
▲ 1 million to 5 million
● 500,000 to 1 million
• Under 500,000

miles
0   100
km
0   100

Orkney Islands

Outer Hebrides

Inner Hebrides

Atlantic Ocean

• Wick

• Inverness

• Aberdeen

HAMMER THROWER, page 45

• Dundee

Glasgow ▲   ● Edinburgh

Londonderry •

Newtownabbey •
Belfast ●

Carlisle •

North Sea

Newcastle-upon-Tyne ▲
Sunderland •

Middlesbrough •

ILLUMINATED TOWER AND STREET DECORATIONS, page 46

Irish Sea

York •

CARNIVAL PARADE, pages 3, 38-39 AND TRYING ARMOR, page 42 AND SHAKESPEARE PLAY, page 47

Blackpool •
Preston •
Bolton •

Bradford •
Blackburn •
Huddersfield •
Leeds ●

Kingston upon Hull •

IRELAND

Liverpool ●
Stockport •
Manchester ▲
Sheffield ▲

Grimsby •

Bangor •

SHOPPING MALL, page 40

Stoke-on-Trent •

Lincoln •

Derby •
Nottingham ●

St. George's Channel

Wolverhampton •
Dudley •
Walsall •
Birmingham ▲
Leicester ●
Peterborough •

Norwich •

Worcester •
Coventry •
Northampton •
Cambridge •

Ipswich •

Milton Keynes •
Cheltenham •
Luton •

Colchester •

Swansea •
Gloucester •
Oxford •

Chelmsford •
Southend-on-Sea •

Newport •
Cardiff ●
Swindon •
Reading •
London ■

Bristol ●
Bath •
Crawley •
Canterbury •

MORRIS DANCERS, page 45

MILLENNIUM STADIUM, page 44

Taunton •
Southampton ●
Brighton ●
Dover •

Exeter •
Poole •
Portsmouth ●
Eastbourne •

Bournemouth •

Plymouth •

English Channel

FRANCE

Penzance •
Truro •

CRICKET MATCH, page 43

Alderney
Guernsey
Jersey

CHANNEL ISLANDS
Scale same as main map.

FRANCE

▲ Indian food is widely available in the United Kingdom. Britons say that their favorite food is "curry"—the name given to spicy Indian sauces.

▼ Students try wearing a crown or armor during a trip to the Tower of London.

Different People

The great majority of people in the United Kingdom are native English, Welsh, Scots, or Irish. They are descendants of the Vikings, Normans, Anglo-Saxons, and others who settled the islands in the past. Today, about 8 percent of the population have very different backgrounds. Half of them are South Asians—from Bangladesh, Pakistan, and India— and about a quarter are Afro-Caribbeans. They first came to the United Kingdom to boost the workforce after World War II.

Growing Up in Britain

All British children have to attend school between the ages of 5 and 16. The school week runs from Monday to Friday, with classes starting at 9:00 in the morning and finishing at 3:15 in the afternoon.

Since 1988 schools in England and Wales have followed a central guide of what to teach; the Scottish system is similar. All British pupils take exams every few years to check their progress. Some people think that these regular tests put too much pressure on young children.

Some children attend afterschool clubs, where they take

LEATHER ON WILLOW

Cricket is Britain's traditional summer sport. Its origins go back centuries, but the modern game dates from the late 1700s. The rules are famously complex—they fill 20 pages in the official rule book. The language used to describe the game can also be baffling. A commentator might say something like: "During a maiden over, the nightwatchman at the crease was out when caught at silly mid-on after being bowled a googly."

The game is played with a hard ball covered in red leather, and with a flat bat made from willow. It is played on an oval field, in the middle of which two wickets—three upright sticks with two horizontal sticks on top—face each other. International matches can last for five days.

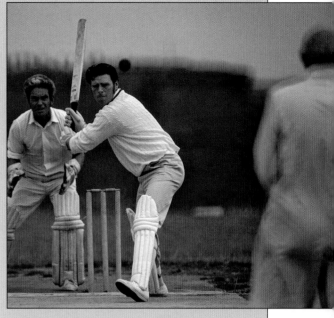

▲ When batting, cricketers wear padding on their legs and hands and other parts of their bodies.

part in sports and other activities. Many are also members of organizations such as the Scouts. Scouting was started in the UK in the early 1900s by Lord Baden Powell and spread around the world.

"On Holiday:" A British Vacation

A favorite British way to relax is to visit the seaside. That can be risky, because the weather there is often bad, so it may be too cold or rainy for the beach. Today people often fly abroad to warmer, sunnier destinations in Europe and America. British seaside resorts are still popular, however, and on weekends many people head for the country for a ramble (hike).

The British also relax by watching sports. Many popular sports began in the United Kingdom, including soccer, rugby, cricket, boxing, and golf. Some sports contests have become social events. They include the Boat Race between Oxford and Cambridge Universities and the tennis championships at Wimbledon. It is traditional for spectators to eat strawberries and cream at Wimbledon. Every year, they go through 27 tons (24,500 kg) of strawberries and 1,850 gallons (7,000 liters) of cream during the two-week competition.

▲ **The Millennium Stadium in Cardiff is the main rugby venue in Wales. Rugby is the Welsh national sport.**

EISTEDDFODS

Every year in Wales, poets, storytellers, musicians, and singers gather to compete in festivals called Eisteddfods (i-steth-vods). These festivals range from small local events to the huge National Eisteddfod in August.

Eisteddfods date back to the Middle Ages. Originally they were competitions held between bards, men who were skilled in performing poetry and music. In later centuries eisteddfods declined, but they became popular again in the 1700s. At this time, Druids—the priests of an ancient British religion—also began taking part. The Archdruid of Gorsedd now presides over the National Eisteddfod.

Peculiar Customs

The UK has a number of festivals that are not celebrated anywhere else in the world. Some are not even celebrated throughout the country. However, one of the national events is Guy Fawkes Night, or Bonfire Night, held on November 5. It marks the day in 1605 when a Roman Catholic named Guy Fawkes tried to blow up Britain's king and Parliament. Today people watch firework displays and light bonfires with a dummy on the top, called a "guy," after Fawkes.

The many regional festivals include the Highland Games in Scotland and morris dancing in England. One unusual local custom is a cheese-rolling event held in Gloucestershire, England. A large, round cheese is rolled off the top of a very steep hill. Competitors hurtle down after it. They often fall, and many end up with broken bones. The first competitor to reach the bottom in one piece gets to keep the cheese!

Britain's newer immigrants have also added a number of festivals to the calendar. They include the

▲ Morris dancers—with bells fitted to their legs—perform at Dover Castle. The roots of morris dancing are uncertain—some suggest it comes from Morocco in Africa.

◄ A hammer thrower, dressed in a traditional kilt, competes at the Highland Games in Glenfinnan.

PUBLIC HOLIDAYS

Most countries have a special day each year when everyone gets the day off to celebrate the nation. The countries of United Kingdom have national days, too, but most people do not get the day off. Only Northern Ireland gets to celebrate its national day with a holiday.

The main public holidays in Britain coincide with New Year, Christmas, and Easter. There are also a number of bank holidays, usually on a Monday. They are called bank holidays because banks are legally allowed to close on these days.

JANUARY 1—New Year's Day
JANUARY 2—Bank holiday in Scotland only as part of Hogmanay—the Scottish New Year celebrations
MARCH 1—Saint David's Day, Wales's national day
MARCH 17—Saint Patrick's Day, national day in Northern Ireland
APRIL 23—Saint George's Day, England's national day
GOOD FRIDAY—Bank holiday
EASTER MONDAY—Bank holiday
FIRST MONDAY IN MAY—May Day bank holiday
LAST MONDAY IN MAY—May bank holiday
FIRST MONDAY IN AUGUST—Bank holiday (Scotland only)
LAST MONDAY IN AUGUST—August bank holiday
NOVEMBER 30—Saint Andrew's Day, Scotland's national day
DECEMBER 25—Christmas Day
DECEMBER 26—Boxing Day

▼ Blackpool is the north of England's most popular beach resort. Its famous tower is a small version of the Eiffel Tower in Paris.

Notting Hill Carnival and Diwali (di-var-lee), the Hindu festival of lights, which is now celebrated in most cities.

Art Old and New

The UK has produced many great writers, including William Shakespeare, Charles Dickens, Dylan Thomas, and Robert Burns. Recently, the English author J.K. Rowling shot to fame with her Harry Potter stories. In 2005 British fans bought 4.1 million copies of *Harry Potter and the Half-Blood Prince*, on the day it was published.

British art ranges from the paintings of the 19th-century

THE GREAT BARD

William Shakespeare (1564–1616) is one of the most famous writers who ever lived. He was born in Stratford-upon-Avon, a town in central England. By the 1590s, he was making a name for himself as a poet and playwright in London. Shakespeare wrote 36 plays, including *Romeo and Juliet* and *A Midsummer Night's Dream*. They are known for their believable characters, their rich language, and their entertaining plots.

Shakespeare introduced many new words to the English language. A tiny selection include: amazement, coldhearted, hot-blooded, moonbeam, nimble-footed, puke, and quarrelsome.

▲ *Julius Caesar* is performed at the New Globe Theatre, a copy of Shakespeare's London theater.

artists John Constable and Joseph Turner to the modern work of Damien Hirst and Tracey Emin. Hirst made his name in the 1990s by displaying preserved dead animals in tanks. Emin is best known for putting her unmade bed on display in a gallery.

British music is just as diverse, ranging from opera to pop. Britain has world-class orchestras and opera stars such as Bryn Terfel. Of course, it has also produced some of the world's most exciting pop music, from the Beatles to punk rock and BritPop.

▼ *Rain, Steam, and Speed–The Great Western Railway* painted by Joseph Turner in 1844.

Pomp
and
Ceremony

EVERY FALL, QUEEN ELIZABETH II opens the new session of Parliament. In a ceremony that dates back centuries, a horse-drawn carriage takes the queen from Buckingham Palace to the Houses of Parliament. She enters the House of Lords to announce the beginning of the process of law-making for the next year. The current queen has opened 53 sessions.

The State Opening of Parliament is a reminder of the traditions that underlie many aspects of British life. The British monarch is not allowed into Parliament's main chamber, the House of Commons. Instead its members are called to the House of Lords to hear her. The last king to enter the Commons was Charles I, in 1642, and he ended up having his head cut off!

◀ Queen Elizabeth II opens Parliament for the year. Her speech outlines the government's aims: It is written for her by the government, and she simply reads it out loud.

PARTY POLITICS

The United Kingdom has three main political parties: the Conservative Party, the Labour Party, and the Liberal Democratic Party. There are also nationalist parties that express the views of many Scottish, Welsh, and Irish voters.

Traditionally, the Conservatives are associated with middle-class values. Labour has closer ties with working-class people and the labor union movement. The Liberal Democrats attempt to win support from both groups.

One of the most unusual political parties is the Monster Raving Loony Party. Its candidates are unlikely to be elected. The party was started as a joke in 1983 by a pop star named Screaming Lord Sutch. He was later replaced as party leader by a cat! Monster Raving Loony candidates fight for many seats in elections—and always lose.

▶ **Most British mayors do not have any power, they just perform ceremonies. Here the Lord Mayor of Oxford walks behind a man carrying a ceremonial mace—a symbol of the mayor's position.**

Trading Partners

More than half of the United Kingdom's trade is with other European countries. The United States is also an important trading partner. Exports include oil, high-tech machinery, and financial services. Imports include food, vehicles, and clothing.

Country	Percentage of exports
United States	14.6%
Germany	10.9%
France	9.4%
Ireland	7.7%
Netherlands	6.0%
All others combined	51.4%

Country	Percentage of imports
Germany	14.0%
United States	7.9%
France	7.9%
Netherlands	7.3%
Belgium	5.4%
All others combined	57.5%

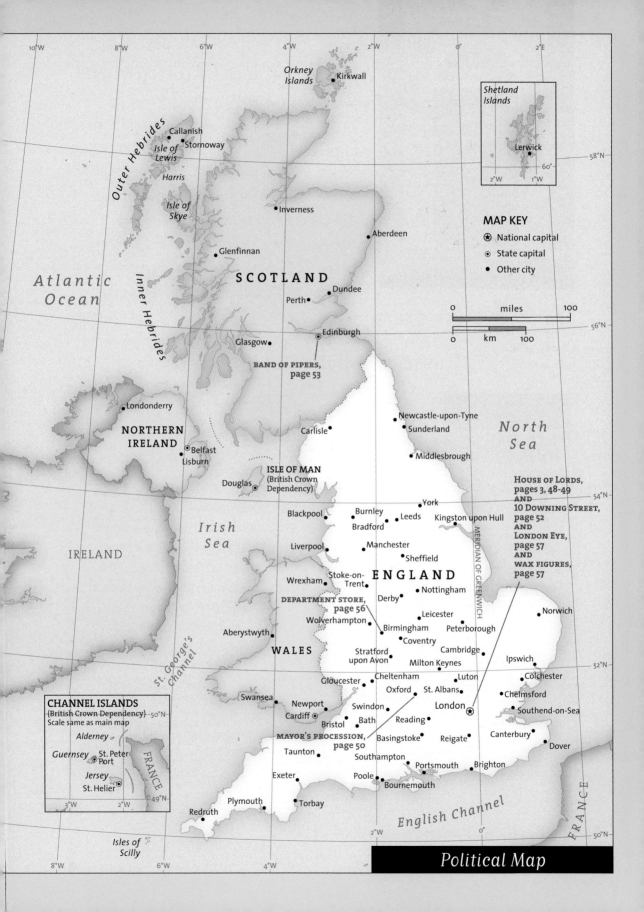

10°W   8°W   6°W   4°W   2°W   0°   2°E

Orkney
Islands   Kirkwall

Callanish
Outer Hebrides   Stornoway
Isle of
Lewis

Harris

Isle of
Skye   Inverness

Aberdeen

SCOTLAND

Dundee
Perth

Glasgow   Edinburgh

BAND OF PIPERS,
page 53

Atlantic
Ocean

Inner Hebrides

Shetland
Islands

Lerwick

60°

2°W   1°W

58°N

MAP KEY

✸ National capital
⊙ State capital
● Other city

0   miles   100

0   km   100

56°N

Londonderry

NORTHERN
IRELAND   Belfast
Lisburn

Douglas

*Irish
Sea*

IRELAND

Newcastle-upon-Tyne
Carlisle   Sunderland

Middlesbrough

*North
Sea*

ISLE OF MAN
(British Crown
Dependency)

York

Blackpool   Burnley   Leeds
Bradford   Kingston upon Hull

Liverpool   Manchester
Sheffield

54°N

HOUSE OF LORDS,
pages 3, 48-49
AND
10 DOWNING STREET,
page 52
AND
LONDON EYE,
page 57
AND
WAX FIGURES,
page 57

Wrexham   Stoke-on-
Trent   ENGLAND   Nottingham

Derby

Norwich

DEPARTMENT STORE,
page 56   Leicester

Wolverhampton   Peterborough

Aberystwyth   Birmingham
Coventry   Cambridge   Ipswich

WALES   Stratford
upon Avon   Milton Keynes   52°N

Colchester

Gloucester   Cheltenham   Luton
Swansea   Oxford   St. Albans   Chelmsford

Newport   Swindon   London   Southend-on-Sea
Cardiff   Bath   Reading

Bristol   Canterbury
MAYOR'S PROCESSION,
page 50   Basingstoke   Reigate   Dover

*St. George's
Channel*

CHANNEL ISLANDS
(British Crown Dependency)
Scale same as main map   50°N

Alderney

Guernsey   St. Peter
Port

Jersey
St. Helier   49°N

3°W   2°W

FRANCE

Taunton   Southampton
Portsmouth   Brighton

Exeter   Poole   Bournemouth

Redruth   Plymouth   Torbay

English Channel

FRANCE

*Isles of
Scilly*   2°W   0°   50°N

8°W   6°W   4°W

Political Map

For King and Parliament

Britain's system of government has developed over many centuries. In the early days, English kings ruled with advice from a council of religious leaders and nobles. This royal council grew in power and was joined by knights—military leaders—from all regions of the country. By the 1300s the nobles in the council had become the House of Lords. The other knights formed the House of Commons. Together they made up Parliament—a name that comes from the French word *parler*, meaning "to speak."

▲ A fox creeps past 10 Downing Street—the home of the UK's prime minister.

HOW THE GOVERNMENT WORKS

The United Kingdom is a constitutional monarchy and a parliamentary democracy. This means that the queen—or king—is the head of state, but the country is run by an elected government. The main parliament is in Westminster, London. After a general election, the political party with the most elected members of Parliament forms the government. That party's leader becomes the prime minister, who appoints a cabinet and runs the country. Any new laws are approved by the queen. Parliament consists of two parts: elected members join the House of Commons; members of the House of Lords are appointed by the main political parties. The House of Lords is also the country's highest court and is overseen by judges called the Law Lords.

THE QUEEN		
EXECUTIVE	LEGISLATIVE	JUDICIARY
PRIME MINISTER	HOUSE OF LORDS (670 MEMBERS)	LAW LORDS
CABINET (25 MINISTERS)	HOUSE OF COMMONS (646 MEMBERS)	HIGH COURT

There were many power struggles between the monarch and Parliament, including a civil war. In 1689 Parliament introduced a Bill of Rights. It made sure that they rather than the monarch would be responsible for passing all new laws.

Figureheads and Leaders

Today's queen has no real power. She must sign all the government's laws before they can come into force, and in theory she could choose not to sign—but no British monarch has dared to do that since 1707.

The government is elected by British people ages 18 and over every five years or so. Each small area, or constituency, elects a member of Parliament (MP) who represents them in London. There are currently 646 MPs in the House of Commons.

The House of Lords has 670 members; they are not elected. A few have inherited the right to the job from their families. However, in 1999 this practice was ended, and new members are now all appointed.

Most members of the Lords belong to political parties, but others are not linked to any party. They

▼ A band of Scottish pipers wearing tartan (a traditional checked material) kilts march outside Edinburgh Castle during the Tatoo, a military parade that takes place in the Scottish capital each August. The Scots, like the Welsh, the Northern Irish, and many English regions, maintain their own cultural traditions.

INDUSTRY MAP

This map shows the location of the United Kingdom's industrial centers. The country has undersea oil and gas fields in its waters, and there are many refineries on the coast. The United Kingdom has few manufacturing industries left, and most mines have become too costly to run.

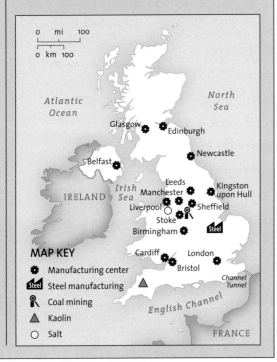

o mi 100
o km 100

Atlantic Ocean

North Sea

Glasgow
Edinburgh
Newcastle
Belfast
Irish Sea
IRELAND
Leeds
Manchester
Kingston upon Hull
Liverpool
Sheffield
Stoke
Birmingham
Steel
Cardiff
London
Bristol
Channel Tunnel
English Channel
FRANCE

MAP KEY

- ✿ Manufacturing center
- Steel — Steel manufacturing
- ⚒ Coal mining
- ▲ Kaolin
- ○ Salt

are known as the crossbenchers, and they sit in the middle of the chamber.

There are not enough seats for everyone in the two halls where the MPs and lords meet. During busy debates, some must stand up or just stay outside.

In the Regions

Until 1707 Scotland had its own Parliament, but it closed when the country merged with England. In 1999 the Scottish Parliament opened again to give Scots more say over their own region. For the first time Wales and Northern Ireland also got their own regional assemblies. These organizations have only limited powers, however.

There are also many levels of local government. The UK is divided into areas that each have an elected council. The councils are responsible for providing services such as schools and housing. The system is very complex, and the organization of regions often changes. As a result some parts of the country are governed in different ways from others. For example, in 2000 the Greater London Authority took over the running of London from 33 borough councils. It is led by Britain's first elected mayor of any city.

Trading Capital

The United Kingdom has been a leading trading nation for more than five hundred years. In the 19th century British industry helped to make the country the most powerful nation in the world.

Today, foreign trade generates about half the United Kingdom's wealth. More than half of all trade is with other European countries. Britain is a member of the European Union (EU), an organization designed to promote cooperation between European nations.

The United Kingdom grew rich by making products and selling them abroad, but today the fastest-growing part of the British economy are the service industries. Instead of manufacturing things, these industries help

THE CITY WITHIN A CITY

The financial district of the city of London is called the City. It is also known as the Square Mile—because that is the area of the district.

The City has long been home to the United Kingdom's most important financial institutions. The Bank of England is there, and so is the Stock Exchange. In the 1980s the City was transformed after a change in the laws on how financial organizations operate. Business boomed, and soon the City was one big construction site. As more and more businesses tried to squeeze into the Square

Mile, office buildings reached upward. These skyscrapers dominate the skyline. They have become London landmarks, including the pickle-shaped tower that everyone calls the Gherkin.

▶ Traders in the City no longer see their customers face-to-face. Instead, they buy and sell stocks and shares through a computer system.

other companies or individuals do the things they need. Service industries include banking, leisure, information technology, communications, and transportation. Three-quarters of all British workers do these jobs.

Nothing to Make

The factories that made Britain wealthy began to close in the late 20th century. After hundreds of years, the supplies of coal and iron ore on which many industries relied began to run out. British workers could no longer make things as cheaply as factories could in other parts of the world.

Other changes in the 1980s had an impact. The government owned and ran many industries. They have now been sold to private buyers. Although the government could support unprofitable mines, shipyards, and automobile plants, private owners would not. Most were shut down, and millions lost their jobs. After several years of high unemployment, the British economy recovered. It is now one of the strongest in the world.

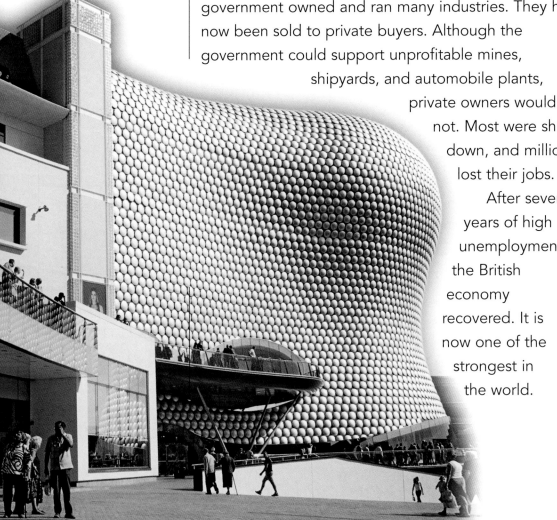

▼ Britain's industrial cities have been redeveloped over the last 20 years. This futuristic structure is a large department store in Birmingham.

THE EYE IN THE SKY

The London Eye is the world's largest ferris wheel. It was built in the capital to celebrate the millennium in 2000. It is 443 feet (135 m) tall and has 32 passenger capsules that give great views of the city in all directions. On a clear day you can see 40 miles (64 km) away. Although it was only meant to be temporary, the Eye's 3.5 million visitors each year make it the United Kingdom's number-one tourist attraction.

Bust and Boom

Although 70 percent of Britain is farmland, today only 2 percent of the population works in agriculture. The fishing industry has also declined. The numbers of fish in the waters around Britain are so low that the EU limits how much fishers can catch.

While some industries decline, others grow. Tourism is now the largest part of the British economy. The UK is one of the ten most-visited countries in the world. About 30 million foreign tourists arrive each year. They include 3.5 million Americans: that's more than the entire population of Wales!

▼ Tourists peek at a letter held by a wax figure of an aristocratic lady from the early 1900s.

Add a Little Extra to Your Country Report!

I f you are assigned to write a report about the United Kingdom, you'll want to include basic information about the country, of course. The Fast Facts chart on page 8 will give you a good start. The rest of the book will give you the details you need to create a full and up-to-date paper or PowerPoint presentation. But what can you do to make your report more fun than anyone else's? If you use your imagination and dig a bit deeper into some of the topics introduced in this book, you're sure to come up with information that will make your report unique!

>Flag

Perhaps you could explain the history of the United Kingdom's flag, and the meanings of its colors and symbols. Go to **www.crwflags.com/fotw/flags** for more information.

>National Anthem

How about downloading the United Kingdom's national anthem, and playing it for your class? At **www.nationalanthems.info** you'll find what you need, including the words to the anthem, plus sheet music for it. Simply pick "U" and then "United Kingdom" from the list on the left-hand side of the screen, and you're on your way.

>Time Difference

If you want to understand the time difference between the United Kingdom and where you are, this Web site can help: **www.worldtimeserver.com**. Just pick "United Kingdom" from the list on the left. If you called someone in the UK right now, would you wake them up from their sleep?

>Currency

Another Web site will convert your money into pounds, the currency used in the United Kingdom. You'll want to know how much money to bring if you're ever lucky enough to travel to the United Kingdom: **www.xe.com/ucc**.

>Weather

Why not check the current weather in the United Kingdom? It's easy—go to **www.weather.com** to find out if it's sunny or cloudy, warm or cold in the United Kingdom right now! Pick "World" from the headings at the top of the page. Then search for the United Kingdom. Click on any city. Be sure to click on the tabs below the weather report for Sunrise/Sunset information, Weather Watch, and Business Travel Outlook, too. Scroll down the page for the 36-hour Forecast and a satellite weather map. Compare your weather to the weather in the UK city you chose. Is this a good season, weather-wise, for a person to travel to the United Kingdom?

>Miscellaneous

Still want more information? Simply go to National Geographic's One-Stop Research site at **http://www.nationalgeographic.com/onestop**. It will help you find maps, photos and art, articles and information, games and features that you can use to jazz up your report.

Glossary

Annul to cancel a marriage. Annulment is different from divorce because it declares that the marriage was never valid rather than simply ending it. Roman Catholics are not allowed to divorce, but may ask the pope to annul their marriages.

Carnival in the United Kingdom, a party that takes place in cities with large Caribbean communities during the summer. People dance, play music, and take part in processions dressed in bright costumes.

Circa about; used to indicate a date that is approximate, and abbreviated as ca.

Colony a region that is ruled by a nation located somewhere else in the world. Settlers from that distant country take the land from the region's original inhabitants.

Conquest a military invasion where a foreign force takes control of, or conquers, new land.

Druid a person who follows the religion of ancient Britons called Celts. Druids dress in white robes, carry a staff, and walk in bare feet. Druids are often depicted in legends and folk tales as mysterious wizards and witches.

Economy the system by which a country creates wealth through making and trading in products.

Ecosystem a community of living things and the environment they interact with; an ecosystem includes plants, animals, soil, water, and air.

Emperor the ruler of an empire.

Figurehead a person who has the job of being in charge of a country or other organization, although he or she does not have any power. The word comes from the figures carved on the prow (front) of many wooden ships.

Financial relating to finance, the management of money by companies, governments and individuals.

Glacier a body of ice formed over thousands of years, mainly by layers of snow, that slowly flows on land.

Hindu a follower of Hinduism, a religion founded in India that involves the worship of many different gods and spirits.

Mainland a larger area of land next to an island.

Monastery an institution where monks live.

Myth a traditional story that is used to explain the origins of culture, such as how or why a country or community came to be formed.

Noble a person with a title given to them by the king or queen. Most British noblemen are known as lords, but they might also be a duke, earl, marquis, or baron. Noblewomen are generally ladies, but some are a dame, countess, or marchioness. Most, but not all nobles, can attend the House of Lords.

Principality a region that is ruled by a prince on behalf of the monarch. In the United Kingdom, the title of Prince of Wales is given to the monarch's eldest son. The Prince of Wales will become the next monarch.

Scandinavia a region of northwestern Europe, which includes Norway, Sweden, and Denmark. Iceland and Finland are sometimes also included. Many of the ancestors of modern British people came from Scandinavia.

Species a type of organism; animals or plants in the same species look similar and can only breed successfully among themselves.

Bibliography

Campbell, Kumari. *United Kingdom in Pictures.* Minneapolis: Lerner Publications Co., 2004.

Woolf, Alex. *Focus on the United Kingdom.* Milwaukee, WI: World Almanac Library, 2007.

http://www.number-10.gov.uk/output/page41.asp (virtual tour of 10 Downing Street)

http://www.parliament.uk/ (official Web site of the UK Parliament)

http://www.royal.gov.uk/ (official Web site of the British monarch)

http://www.visitbritain.com/ (general information)

Further Information

NATIONAL GEOGRAPHIC Articles

Kelly, Patrick, J. "London Calling." NATIONAL GEOGRAPHIC TRAVELER (April 2007): 64–73, 108.

O'Neill, Tom. "Celt Appeal." NATIONAL GEOGRAPHIC (March 2006): 74–95.

Yeadon, David. "Britain Coast to Coast." NATIONAL GEOGRAPHIC TRAVELER (July/ August 2002): 82–94.

Web sites to explore

More fast facts about the United Kingdom, from the CIA (Central Intelligence Agency): https://www.cia.gov/cia/publications/factbook/geos/uk.html

The United Kingdom has the world's largest broadcaster, the British Broadcasting Corporation, or BBC. Visit the BBC Web site to watch British TV shows, listen to the radio, download podcasts, or read the archive of news stories: http://www.bbc.co.uk

Stonehenge and many other monuments and old buildings are managed by English Heritage. Search this Web site to find out more about historic sites: http://www.english-heritage.org.uk

The Tower of London is one of several Royal Palaces. Look at this site to find out how many jewels are in the Queen's crown and see where Princess Diana used to live: http://www.hrp.org.uk/

Want to know more about life at Hadrian's Wall? Try the Kid's Zone of the official Web site and play this fun game: http://www.hadrians-wall.org/kids_zone.aspx

See, hear

There are many ways to get a taste of life in the United Kingdom, such as movies, music, magazines, or TV shows. You might be able to locate these:

The Queen (2006)
A movie about the reaction to the death of Princess Diana in 1997. Helen Mirren won an Oscar for her role as Queen Elizabeth II.

First News
This is the first newspaper in Britain written just for children. Read the latest issue at http://www.firstnews.co.uk

Blue Peter
One of the longest-running children's shows, *Blue Peter* has been broadcast for nearly 50 years. See clips from the latest shows at http://www.bbc.co.uk/cbbc/bluepeter/

Index

Boldface indicates illustrations.

Angles 28–29
Anglesey 11
Anglo-Saxons 29, 42
architecture **32**, **34**, **56**
Armada 32
Augustine, Saint 29

badgers 22, **22**
Bass Rock 21
Beatles 47
Belfast 8
Ben Nevis 8
Birmingham 15, **15**, **56**
Black Death 30–31
Blackpool **46**
bluebells **22**
Boat Race 44
Bonfire Night 44–45
British Empire 7, 32, 35–36, **35**,
    36, 37
BritPop 47
Broads 14, **14**
Burnley **36**
Burns, Robert 46

Cambridge 8
canals 15, **15**, **36**
Canute 30
Cardiff 8
    Millennium Stadium **44**
Carnival **38–39**
castles **29**, 30, **30**, **45**
cathedrals **31**
Celts 6, 28–29
chalk pictures 13, **13**
Charles I 33, 49
Charles II 33
cheese-rolling 45
Christianity 28, 29, 31, **31**,
    32–33
cities 15, 23, 36, 40
City, the 55, **55**
civil war, English 33, 53
climate 8, 43
coal 15, 56
coastline 14–15, 20–21
Columba, Saint 29

conservation organizations 18
Constable, John 47
Cornwall **10**, **12**, **23**, 29
Cotswold Hills 7
cricket 43, **43**
Crimean War 35

deer **16–17**, 17, **20**, 22
Dickens, Charles 46
diet **42**
Diwali 46
Dover Castle **45**
Druids 21, 44
Dunwich 14–15

East Anglia 14, **14**
economy 55–57
Eden Project **23**
Edinburgh 8, **53**
education 42–43, 54
Edward VI 33
Eisteddfods 44
Elizabeth I 31–32, 33
Elizabeth II **35**, **48**
Emin, Tracey 47
England 10–11, 13, 25
English language 8, 30

Falkland Islands War **37**
farming **11**, 12, 57
Farne Islands **18**
Fens 8, 14
fishing industry 57
flood defenses 15, **15**
Forest of Dean 21
forests and woodland 21, 22, **22**
foxes 22, 23, **52**

Gaelic language 11
George I 34
Georgian period 34, **34**
Giant's Causeway 10, **10**
Glasgow 40
glens 17
Globe Theatre **47**
Glorious Twelfth 20
golden eagle 20
grouse 20
Guy Fawkes Night 44–45

Hadrian's Wall 29, **29**
Hanoverians 26
Harris 11
heather 20
Hebrides 11, **11**
Henry VII 31
Henry VIII 31–32, **32**, 33
Highland Games 45, **45**
Hirst, Damien 47
Holy Island **29**
Hood, Robin 21

immigration 42, 45–46
Industrial Revolution 26, 35–36,
    36, 40
Ireland 11, 25, 37
iron ore 15, 56
islands 10–11, **10**, **11**
Isle of Wight 11

James I 32
Jutes 28

Lake District **1**, 12–13
lakes 8, 12–13
Lerwick **24–25**, 25
Lewis 11, **11**
Lindisfarne Castle **29**
Liverpool **40**
Loch Ness 13
lochs 13
London **6–7**, 7, 8, 23, 40, 54, 55
    London Eye 57, **57**
    Thames Barrier 15, **15**
    Tower Bridge **6–7**
    Tower of London **30**, 42
Lundy 11

maps
    Falkland Islands 37
    historical **27**
    industry **54**
    physical **9**
    political **51**
    population **41**
    vegetation and ecosystems **19**
    weather and climate **8**
Mary I 31
Millennium Stadium **44**

mining 15, 54
monarchy 8, 26, 31–34, **48**, 49, 52–53
moors 20, **20**
morris dancing 45, **45**
mountains 8, **9**, 12–13, **12**, 20
Mourne 12

National Parks 18
navy 21, 32
Newcastle-upon-Tyne 15
Nightingale, Florence **35**
Normans 26, 30, **30**, 42
Northern Ireland 10–11, 37, 54
Notting Hill Carnival **38–39**, 39, 45–46

oak trees 21, **21**
oil and gas fields 54
Orkney 11
Osmington White Horse **13**
Oxford University **5**

Parliament 8, 34, 36, **48–49**, 49, 52–54
Patrick, Saint 29
peat 14
Picts 6, 28
political system 50–54
pollution 18
population 8, 40–42, **40**, **41**
   map **41**
puffins **18**
punk rock 47
Puritans 33

rabbits 23
rivers 8
road system 6
Romans 26, **27**, 28, 29, **29**
Rowling, J. K. 46
royal family
   Saxe-Coburg-Gotha 26
   Stuarts 26
   Tudors 26, 31–32
   Windsors 26
rugby 44, **44**

St. Kilda 11
St. Michael's Mount **10**
Salisbury Cathedral **31**
Saxe-Coburg-Gotha 26
Saxons 26, 28–29
Scoti 28
Scotland 10–11, **20**, 25, **53**, 54
Scottish Highlands 12, 13, **16**, 17, 20
seagulls 21
seals 21
Severn River 15
Shakespeare, William 46, 47, **47**
Sherwood Forest 21
Shetland 11, **24–25**, 25
Snowdonia 12, **12**
sports 43, **43**, 44, **44**
Square Mile 55, **55**
squirrels 22
Staffa 10
Stornoway 8
Stratford-upon-Avon 47
Stuarts 26
Swansea 15

tartan **53**
Tatoo **53**
10 Downing Street 52
Terfel, Bryn 47
Thames Barrier 15, **15**
Thames River **6–7**, 7, 8, 15
Thatcher, Margaret 37
Thomas, Dylan 46
time line **26**
tourism 57, **57**
Tower Bridge **6–7**, 7
Tower of London **30**, 42
trade 50, 55–56
Tudors 26, 31–32
Turner, Joseph 47, **47**
tweed 11, **20**

Uffington White Horse 13
United Kingdom 25
Up Helly-Aa **24–25**, 25

vacations 43–44
vegetation and ecosystems 18, **19**, 20–23
Victoria, Queen 35
Vikings 25, 26, 30, 42
Wales 10–11, 25, 29, 54
Wars of the Roses 31
Welsh language 8, 40
wildlife 17–23
   endangered species 18
Wimbledon 44
windmills 14, **14**
Windsors 26
wool 7, 11
World War I 36
World War II 13, 36

Credits

Picture Credits

NGIC = National Geographic Image Collection

Front Cover – Spine: Keith Levit/Shutterstock; Top: Annie Griffiths Belt/NGIC; Low far left: Jodi Cobb/NGIC; Low left: Jim Richardon/NGIC; Low right: Jim Richardon/NGIC; Low far right: Richard Nowitz/NGIC.

Interior – Corbis: Atlantide Phototravel: 40 lo; Niall Benvie 2 right, 16–17; Bettmann: 35 up; Russell Boyce/Reuters: 3 right, 48–49; David Cheshire/Loop Images: 22 lo; Paul Hardy: 2 left, 6–7; Stephen Hird/Reuters: 52 up; Philippa Lewis: 56 lo; O. Louis Mazzatenta: 15 lo, 50 lo; National Gallery Collection; By kind permission of the Trustees of the National Gallery, London: 47 lo; Roger Tidman: 14 center; John Westrich/zefa: 59 up; NGIC: James L. Amos: 43 up; Jonathan Blair: 30 up, 30 lo, 32 lo, 42 lo;Ira Block: 13 lo; Victor R. Boswell, Jr: 33 up; Jodi Cobb: 3 left, 38–39, 47 up, 55 lo; Bill Curtsinger: 29 up; Nicole Duplaix: 57 up; Martin Gray: 29 lo; Annie Griffiths Belt: TP, 5 up; Gideon Mendel: 34 lo; George F. Mobley: 15 up, 21 up, 46 lo; Vincent J. Musi: 44 up; Richard Nowitz: 22 up, 31 up, 57 lo; Steve Raymer: 37 up, 42 up; Jim Richardson: 10 up, 10 lo, 11 up, 12 up, 12 lo, 23 lo, 28 centre, 45 lo, 53 lo; James L. Stanfield: 26 center; Tomasz Tomaszewski: 45 up; Cary Wolinsky 18 lo, 20 center, 36 lo; Adam Woolfitt: 2–3, 24–25; Michael S. Yamashita: 32 up; Paul Zahl: 35 lo.

Text copyright © 2007 National Geographic Society
Published by the National Geographic Society.
All rights reserved. Reproduction of the whole or any part of the contents without written permission from the National Geographic Society is strictly prohibited. For information about special discounts for bulk purchases, contact National Geographic Special Sales: ngspecsales@ngs.org

For more information, please call 1-800-NGS-LINE (647-5463) or write to the following address:

NATIONAL GEOGRAPHIC SOCIETY
1145 17th Street N.W.
Washington, D.C. 20036-4688 U.S.A.

Visit the Society's Web site at www.nationalgeographic.com

Library of Congress Cataloging-in-Publication Data available on request
ISBN: 978-1-4263-0126-1

Printed in the United States of America

Series design by Jim Hiscott.
The body text is set in Avenir; Knockout.
The display text is set in Matrix Script.

Front Cover—Top: A reflection of London's Westminster Abbey in a taxi cab; Low Far Left: Telephone booths, London; Low Left: Highland sheep grazing in Glencoe, Scotland; Low Right: Bagpipers, Edinburgh; Low Far Right: Twilight view of Stonehenge

Page 1—A shepherd and his sheep in the Lake District in northern England; Icon image on spine, Contents page, and throughout: Coldstream Guards

Produced through the worldwide resources of the National Geographic Society

John M. Fahey, Jr., *President and Chief Executive Officer*; Gilbert M. Grosvenor, *Chairman of the Board*; Nina D. Hoffman, *Executive Vice President, President of Book Publishing Group*

National Geographic Staff for this Book

Nancy Laties Feresten, *Vice President, Editor-in-Chief of Children's Books*
Bea Jackson, *Director of Design and Illustration*
David M. Seager, *Art Director*
Virginia Koeth, *Project Editor*
Lori Epstein, *Illustrations Editor*
Stacy Gold, Nadia Hughes, *Illustrations Research Editors*
Priyanka Lamichhane, *Assistant Editor*
R. Gary Colbert, *Production Director*
Lewis R. Bassford, *Production Manager*
Maryclare Tracy, Nicole Elliott, *Manufacturing Managers*
Maps, *Mapping Specialists, Ltd.*

Brown Reference Group plc. Staff for this Book

Volume Editor: Tom Jackson
Designer: Dave Allen
Picture Manager: Clare Newman
Maps: Martin Darlinson
Artwork: Darren Awuah
Index: Ann Barrett
Senior Managing Editor: Tim Cooke
Design Manager: Sarah Williams
Children's Publisher: Anne O'Daly
Editorial Director: Lindsey Lowe

About the Author

RACHEL BEAN is a British author who specializes in cultural studies and the history of art. She has written or edited many books and has also contributed articles to a wide range of encyclopedias. When she is not on her frequent travels to different parts of the world, she lives in Shropshire, a beautiful rural area near the border between England and Wales.

About the Consultants

ROBERT BENNETT is Professor of Geography at the University of Cambridge, United Kingdom. He is an economic geographer who specializes in local economic development in Britain and Europe, the evolution of small firms, and the role of skills and entrepreneurism. He has published many books and research papers on the British economy, including *Local and Regional Economic Development* (2000, with Diane Payne). He is a fellow of the British Academy.

MICHAEL DUNFORD is a professor of economic geography at the University of Sussex, United Kingdom. His research focuses on European economic, regional, and urban geography. He has published a number of books and numerous papers. In 2003 he was awarded the Royal Geographical Society's Edward Heath Award for geographical research in Europe.